COOK

EAT

DEATH METAL

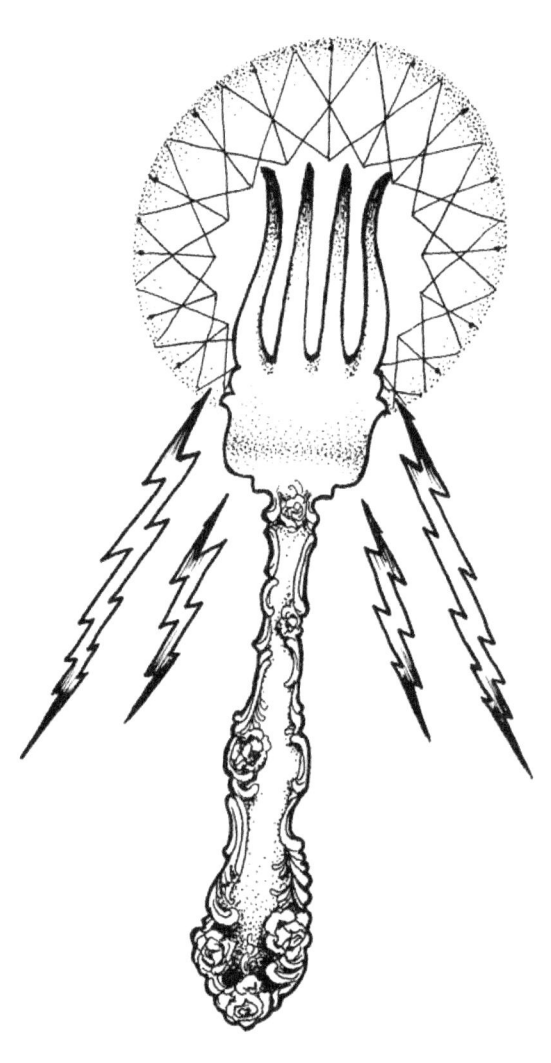

Cook, Eat, Death Metal

A badass rock and roll recipe book celebrating
the deliciousness that is
Eagles of Death Metal

Written by Leslie Bilderback
Cover Art by Shannon O'Sullivan
Photos by Teri Lyn Fisher
Supported by Dissention Records
and Artist Management

Published By Leslie Bilderback
2016

First Printing: 2016

ISBN # 978-1-4575-5066-9

For inquires please visit the following
For distribution: www.Dissentionrecords.com
For cover art: ShannonO'SullivanTatoo@Instagram and
RoseFord@Instagram
For photography: www.terilynfisher.com
For culinary advice: www.culinarymasterclass.com

This book is dedicated to the people of Paris, and to the memories, families, and friends of the victims of the Bataclan Massacre, November 13, 2016.

Alban Denuit
Alberto Gonzales Garrido
Anne Guyomard
Antoine Mary
Ariane Theiller
Armelle Pumir Anticevic
Aurélie de Peretti
Baptiste Chevréau
Bertrand Navarret
Caroline Prénat
Cécile Martin
Cécile Misse
Cédric Gomet
Cédric Mauduit
Christophe Foultier
Christophe Lellouche
Christophe Mutez
Christopher Neuet Shalter Bodineau
Claire Camax
Claire Maitrot-Tapprest
David Perchirin
Elodie Breuil
Elsa Veronique Delplace
Emmanuel Bonnet
Eric Thomé
Estelle Rouat
Fabian Stech
Fabrice Dubois
Fanny Minot
Franck Pitiot
François-Xavier Prévost
Frederic Henninot
Germain Ferey
Gilles Leclerc
Gregory Fosse
Guilaume Decherf
Helene Muyal
Hugo Sarrade
Isabelle Merlin
Jean-Jacques Amiot
Jean-Jacques Kirchheim
Juan Alberto-González Garrido Julien Galisson
Lola Ouzounian

Lola Salines
Luis Felipe Zschoche Valle
Madeleine Sadin
Manu Perez
Marion Jouanneau
Marie Lausch
Marie Mosser
Mathias Dymarski
Mathieu Hoche
Matthieu Rorthais
Matthieu Giroud
Maud Serrault
Maxime Bouffard
Mayeul Gaubert
Nathalie Jardin
Nathalie Lauraine
Nick Alexander
Nicolas Classeau
Olivier Vernadal
Patricia San Martin Nunez
Pierre Innocenti
Pierre Yves
Pierre-Antoine Henry
Précilia Correia
Quentin Boulenger
Quentin Mourier
Renaud Le Guen
Richard Rammant
Romain Dunet
Romain Naufle
Salah Emad El-Gebaly
Stephane Albertini
Stephane Hache
Suzon Garrigues
Sven Alejandro
Silva Perugini
Raphäel Ruiz
Thibault Rousse
Lacordaire Thomas Ayad
Thomas Duperron
Valentin Ribet
Valeria Solc̣in
Vincent Detoc
William B. Decherf
Yannick Minvielle

Table of Contents

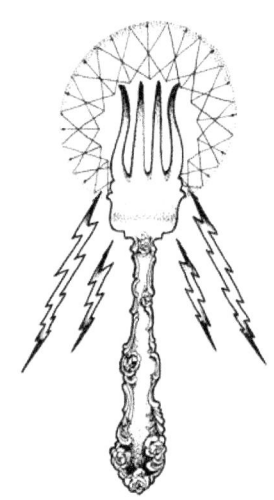

Welcome to the Rock and Roll kitchen.

Here you will find serious recipes, written by a serious
chef who is also a serious fan.
Don't be fooled by their asinine titles.
These recipes are legit.

More than legit. They're fucking amazing.

This project began with a few funny recipes designed to
cheer up a group of fans after the attack on Paris, November 13, 2015. When tragedy strikes, sometimes you
just need to laugh. And eat. This book is a continuation
of that idea. Proceeds from sales are being directed to
The Sweet Stuff, a foundation that supports the musical
community when in need. The Sweet Stuff spearheaded
Paris relief funding, and will continue to do so with
your help.

Thanks for buying this book!

Rock On!

Opening Acts

Starters. Snacks.

In the world of rock and roll, a snack or appetizer typically involves a tube of Pringles and a cigarette. But somewhere along the great highway of life, you might decide to put forth some type of effort. If you find yourself at the crossroads of Slacker Street and Bon Vivant Boulevard, then this chapter is for you.

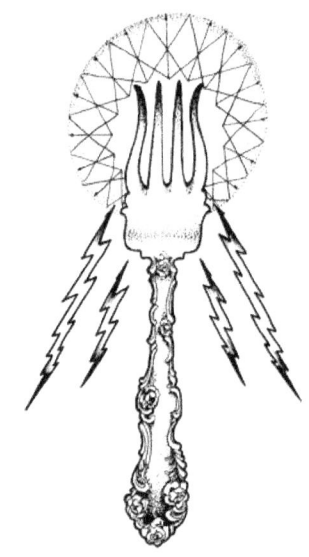

I Only Want Choux

(I Only Want You, *Peace Love Death Metal*, 2004)

Pâte a choux (referred to simply as "choux" by real chefs), is the dough used to make a fuck ton of classic French dishes, both sweet and savory. Cream Puffs, Éclairs, Croquembouche, and even Churros are all born from this tasty pasty. These **Gougère** are the classic French cheese puffs from Burgundy. Not Ron Burgundy. Burgundy, France, where they nibble these as they sip their great wines. And then they screw.

Ingredients

- 2 cups water
- 5 ounces (1 ¼ stick) unsalted butter
- 1 tablespoon sugar
- 1 teaspoon sea salt
- 1 ⅔ cup all-purpose flour
- 7 eggs
- 1 ½ cup grated Gruyere cheese — *The French adore this cheese, even though it's from Switzerland. I know it doesn't have holes, but trust me, it's Swiss. You can sub generic Swiss cheese in a pinch.*
- ¼ cup minced chives
- 1 extra egg for egg wash

Method

1. Combine water, butter, sugar and salt in a large saucepan and bring it to a boil. At the boil, add the flour and beat it hard (heh heh) for three minutes over high heat. This will be difficult, but just tough it out. Please do not whine about it. Deliciousness, like beauty, sometimes requires sacrifice. Three minutes of stirring is crucial, or the flour will not be properly absorbed, the gluten in the flour will not be activated, and your puffs will not puff, which would totally suck the butt. The mixture should resemble mashed potatoes when ready. *(Do not use a wooden spoon—they have a tendency to snap in half during this stage. Use metal. HEAVY METAL.)*

2. Remove from the heat, cool about 5 minutes, then add the eggs, stirring them in one at a time. I always do this by hand, which is hard, but totally worth it. Lazy

cooks take it to a mixer for this part, but that's lame.
The mixer over-works the dough, and overworked dough
doesn't hold it shape properly when you're trying to
shape puffs or éclairs or whatever. Stirring by hand
yields better product, makes you a badass, and sends you
into a zen-like oneness with the cooking process. So
tough it out. It's ok to rest in between eggs for a minute if you must. Add all 7 eggs—one by one. Finally,
fold in the cheese and chives. Now you're ready to bake!
Rest for a minute if you're tired. Maybe get a drink of
water, or a moist cloth.

3. Preheat the oven to 425°F (220°C), and line a baking
sheet with a piece of parchment paper. Use a tiny ice
cream scooper, or two teaspoons, and scoop walnut-size
wads of dough onto the prepared pan, about 1 inch apart.
Fill up the whole pan. You'll probably need to do this
in a couple of batches. Whisk up that extra egg with a
pinch of salt and brush it lightly over the puffs so
they brown nicely, then pop them into the oven. Bake for
20 minutes, then rotate the pan and bake another 10
minutes, or until they are dark golden brown, firm, and
well risen—(like a good man). If they are not golden and
firm they will deflate once cooled. If they don't look
ready, reduce the heat to 350°F and continue to bake until they are. Repeat with remaining dough.

Now enjoy these cheese puffs of love with someone special—which might just be you—because let's face it…
you're the BEST!

Variations:
Omit the cheese and chives and you have a standard cream
puff. Or, if you pipe it in the shape of a big dick, you
have an éclair. Fill them with luscious whipped cream,
pastry cream, or chocolate mousse, then slather them in
chocolate, and go to town. TO TOWN!

The Salad of Queen Bee and Baby Duck
(The Ballad of Queen Bee and Baby Duck,
Death by Sexy, 2006)

Ever wonder where Mr. Homme's nickname "Baby Duck" origi-
nated? As it turns out, the name was born when Josh and
Jesse were in high school. Babysitting for extra cash,
the two junior rockers were entertaining their charges
with a game of *Duck, Duck, Goose*. Unhappy with the way
the game was progressing, the oldest child became agi-
tated, picked up his youngest sibling and threw her
across the room toward the tall red-headed sitter. Jesse, in an effort to warn his babysitting buddy, shouted
out "Baby! Duck!" Josh's reflexes were quick, and he
ducked just in time to save his ginger quaff from certain damage. The nickname stuck. Now you can celebrate
that history with a **Roasted Duck Salad with Honey Mustard Vinaigrette.**

Ingredients

- ½ small red onion, sliced
- 2 tablespoons honey
- 1 tablespoon Dijon mustard
  1 small shallot, chopped
- 1 teaspoon herbs de Provence or dried thyme
- Grated zest and ¼ cup juice of 1 orange
- 1 tablespoon balsamic vinegar
- ¼ cup olive oil
- 1 cup fresh ripe raspberries—*if they aren't
  available, use fresh frozen berries, de-
  frosted*
- 3 cups shredded roast duck meat *(Use leftovers from Baby Duck recipe on page 21, go
  out for Chinese food and order extra Peking
  Duck or buy duck breasts and roast them at
  400° F for 15-20 min)*
- 1 small red bell pepper, roasted and sliced
  thinly- *yellow or orange peppers are fine to
  use, but don't use a green one. Green peppers taste like cockass, and should only be
  used in Sad Town.*
- 1 Persian or English cucumber, sliced thinly
  *— if all you can find is a regular, fat,
  dildo of a cucumber, peel the waxy skin off*

- 3 cups of mixed fresh greens — *buy a pre-sorted, pre-washed bag if you are a lazy fuck, or make your own mix using Boston lettuce, arugula, watercress, or mache*
- ¼ cup Italian parsley leaves — *pick these off their stems*
- ½ cup toasted walnut pieces

Method

1. Cover the sliced onions in cold water and set aside. This method removes the harsh oils that make raw onions unpleasant for those faced with your dank stank onion breath.

2. In a large bowl whisk together the honey, mustard, shallot, and herbs. Add the orange zest and juice, and vinegar. Slowly drizzle in the olive oil while whisking. Add the raspberries and smush them a little with a fork. This releases their juice and pinks the dressing up.

3. To the dressing bowl add the duck meat, roasted pepper, cucumber, and greens. Toss to coat thoroughly, then transfer to a serving platter. Top with parsley, walnuts, and serve.

"Now the two are complete, and they rule the whole show."

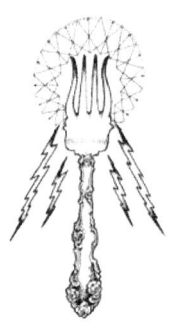

Shasta Yeast
(Shasta Beast, Death by Sexy, 2006)

A great song deserves an exceptional yeasty feasty.
This recipe is for a **California-Style Focaccia**, known as
Focaccia Jardinière in the South of France, because La-
Dee-Fuckin'-Dah. Why a French version, you ask? Just a
little tip of the toque.

Now a word on bread baking: It's fucking easy. Chefs
that proudly exclaim, for instance, on a nationally
broadcast travel/food TV show, that they "don't bake"
because it's "too scientific" are full of shit. A big
fucknugget of shit. First, baking is no more scientific
than grilling a chicken. All the same principles are at
work—just in a different form. (Fats melt, proteins so-
lidify, moisture evaporates, blah blah blah.) And you
can absolutely, 100%, indubitably bake without preci-
sion. It works just as well when you level the cup of
flour as when you eyeball it. Granted, it will not come
out the same every time this way. But most people don't
have a loyal customer base to satisfy with standardiza-
tion. Most people are cooking for one dude on a couch in
his underwear. And that couch dude would be totally
psyched if you decided to start baking. He gives zero
fucks if you level your teaspoon.

This theory of baking is as rock and roll as cooking
gets. Fuck the establishment! Just because someone is
very tall and on TV doesn't mean he's right! (He does
have excellent taste in music, though.) This will make 4
individual focaccia — so you can invite 2 more dudes to
your couch.

Ingredients

- 1 cup warm water — *don't worry about the
  temperature. It should be warm to the touch,
  but you should be able to hold your finger
  in it without screaming. This is slightly
  above body temperature, unless you are extra
  hot.*
- 1 tablespoon honey
- 1 ¾ teaspoon active dry yeast (1 package) -
  *use rapid rise if you like, it matters not a
  shitbit*
- ½ cup whole-wheat flour

- 1 cup olive oil, divided
- 3 teaspoons good sea salt
- 1 ½ - 2 cups bread flour or all-purpose flour
- 2 tablespoons cornmeal
- 2 cups arugula, chopped, washed, and dried
- 2 cups chard, chopped, washed, and dried
- 1 cup kale, chopped, washed, and dried - *Yes kale. Shut up! It's good. It wasn't invented by dumbass hipsters. It's been food for a long time.*
- 1 clove garlic, minced
- Grated zest and juice of ½ lemon
- A bit more olive oil and salt to finish

Method

1. In a large bowl stir together water, honey, yeast, and set aside until foamy, about 5 minutes. Use a fork to stir in the whole-wheat flour to create a loose batter. *(The fork is key here, because it is easy to clean. A whisk just gets jammed up with dough wads.)* Cover and set aside in a warm spot until it begins to bubble, 45-60 minutes. This is the sponge. The sponge is a pre-dough that starts the fermentation process. Fermentation is when yeast feeds on carbs, and releases two by-products. The largest release is carbon dioxide gas. It is literally farting fungi. (Yeast is the fungus among us.) The smaller by-product is alcohol. (Brewers yeast does the same thing, but releases more alcohol, and less CO_2.) The alcohol gets more intense the longer the dough ferments, which is what makes sourdough sour. Incidentally—California's Gold Rush era became famous for sourdough. But the miner 49ers weren't baking. They were drinking the top layer of alcohol off their starters. What they lacked in scruples they made up for in ingenuity.

2. Add to the sponge ½ cup of olive oil, 1 teaspoon of sea salt, and enough bread flour to create a loose dough. (Incidentally, Loose Dough was my nickname in high school.) Turn out onto a floured surface and knead, adding flour only as necessary to reduce stickiness. (!!!!) *This is an important bit here. Don't add all the flour at once. You may need more or less flour depending on several variables, such as weather, brand of flour, or user error. Add ½ cup at a time until it is knead-*

able, then add only a little on your hands to reduce stickiness as necessary. The final dough should be soft, pliable, and easy to knead.

Knead 8-10 minutes, until the dough becomes smooth and elastic. *Knead like a rock star. Really work it! If you can dance for three hours at an EODM concert you can do this for 10 minutes. The gluten needs the agitation to activate its magic elasticity, which is needed for a good rise.* At 8-10 minutes the dough should be tight and smooth, like your favorite ass. Return to the bowl, cover with a warm damp towel, and set aside to rise until doubled in volume, about 1 hour.

3. Preheat oven to 450° F. Coat two baking sheets lightly with olive oil or pan spray, then sprinkle evenly with cornmeal. *(This keeps it from sticking, and gives the finished bread the illusion of having been cooked in a hearth oven. It's just for show, so you can skip it if you don't feel like being a liar.)* Turn risen dough out onto floured surface, and divide into four equal portions. Flatten each portion into ½-inch thick discs. This will take a few minutes, as the elastic dough will spring back a bit. Shape it, let it rest, then shape it again, until it is the size you want. Place the dough on sheet pans (2 per pan), brush the surface with olive oil, and sprinkle with salt. Cover with plastic wrap and set aside for 10 minutes to *proof.* Proof is just another term for fermentation. The dough will get poofy, and just a little larger. When it's a little larger, it's ready. (And that, my friends, is what she said.)

Meanwhile, toss the salad greens and garlic with a tablespoon of olive oil, lemon zest and juice, and generous pinch of salt.

4. Unwrap the proofed dough and top each with the dressed arugula salad. Bake until the dough is golden brown and the greens are singed, about 10-20 minutes. Rotate pan as needed to promote even cooking. Serve immediately with a final pinch of salt.

Variations, because everyone should march to the beat of their own goddamn drummer:
- *Sweet Plain Jane — This bread, without the salad, is equally heavenly. Add a fresh grating of your favorite hard cheese as it comes out of the oven.*

(By the way, "Hard Cheese" is the title of my Au-
tobiography.)

- Sandwich — It is easy to make this bread into a sandwich loaf. Press the entire recipe into a rectangular brownie pan (9x13), then bake per instructions, minus the greens. When cool, cut in half horizontally with a good serrated knife.
- Pizza - Using this dough for pizza is culinarily frowned upon, but fuck those guys. It makes a damn fine pizza pie.

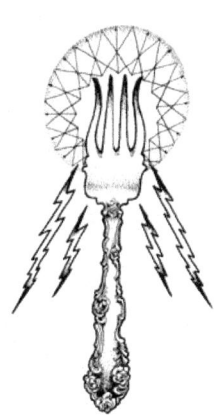

Poor Corn Doggie
(Poor Doggie, Death by Sexy, 2006)

Spicy Corn Dog Poppers are the ultimate bar food. In fact, if you are looking for a job as head chef at T.G.I.Fridays, or the ESPN Fun Zone, this is what you should make for your audition.

Ingredients

- 6-8 large jalapenos — *or more...you need one pepper per popper, a pabulum that is positively pantastic (pardon)*
- ¼ cup chèvre *(that's goat cheese, Einstein)*, chopped fresh mozzarella, or any soft cheese
- 1 package of good hot dogs, such as Nathans!
- 6-8 Skewers — *soak in water for at least 15 minutes*
- 2 tablespoons cornstarch
- 1 ½ cup cornmeal
- ½ cup self-rising flour
- 2 tablespoons granulated sugar
- 1 ¼ cup buttermilk
- Frying oil

Method

1. Slice the stem top off of each jalapeno, and scoop out the seeds. - *Use gloves. The capsicum (aka hotsy-totsy stuff) of the pepper spreads by touch, and it burns. If you don't use gloves, definitely don't pee barehanded afterwards.*

2. Stuff the pepper about 1/3 full with cheese. On top of the cheese insert your wiener. ☺. Insert the skewer through the meat, towards the tip of the pepper.

3. Sift the cornstarch, use it to coat the stuffed peppers, then tap off the excess.

4. In a large bowl combine cornmeal, flour, and sugar, then stir in buttermilk.

5. Fill a heavy pot with 4-5 inches of oil and heat to 375°F. Hold the wieners by their sticks, dip them into the batter, then drop carefully into the oil. Cook for 3-5 minutes, until golden brown all over. Remove from

the oil onto a paper-towel lined tray to drain and cool
slightly. Repeat with remaining wieners. Serve warm with
really good mustard. Frankly, these are fantastic.

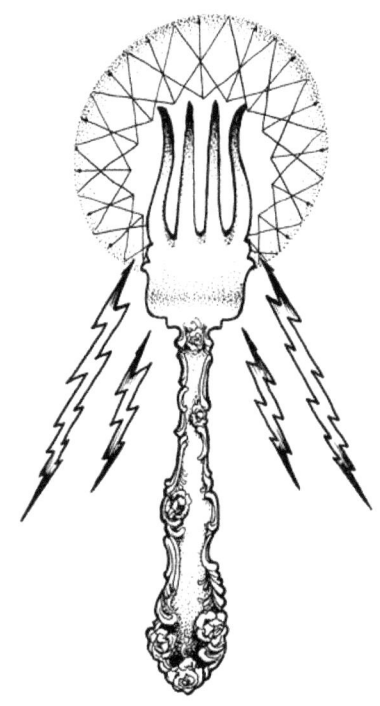

Solo Bites
(Solo Flights, *Heart On,* 2008)

These **Kick Ass Canapés** are going to revolutionize your drinking parties. But let's face it — anything not Doritos will revolutionize your drinking parties.

Ingredients

- 1 cup Italian parsley, chopped
- 1 cup watercress or baby spinach, chopped
- ¼ cup chopped chives
- 1 teaspoon sea salt
- 2 anchovy filets
- 8 ounces unsalted butter, softened at room temperature
- 1 loaf pumpernickel bread, sliced *(use small cocktail loaves or large sandwich loaves cut into smaller pieces—one or two bites each)*
- Very thinly sliced cucumber, radish, and tomato
- Cooked and thinly sliced meat and fish — try ham, roast chicken, whole shrimp, smoked salmon, or hard boiled egg
- Sour cream or crème fraiche
- Caviar—*(if you can swing it)*
- Small sprigs of chervil, dill, or other delicate herb

Method

1. Combine the parsley, watercress, and chives. Add salt, anchovy filets, and mince into a paste. Combine with the softened butter and stir together until soft, smooth, and completely green.

2. Spread small slices of bread with the butter, then begin stacking with your canapé toppings. Start with smooth flat items for structural stability (cucumber slices and hardboiled egg slices, thin tomato slices, radish slices). Top with meat, rolled, folded, or set gently top. Finish with a small dot of sour cream, a few caviar eggs, and a small sprig of herb. Place on a platter, and keep chilled until you're ready to serve.

Wasabi in LA
(Wannabe in LA, *Heart On*, 2008)

Wasabi Guacamole with Wonton Chips is a particularly eyeball-rolling example of stereotypical Southern Californian cuisine. The rest of the world assumes we Angelenos eat avocados everyday. They're right! In fact, the State constitution mandates that California citizens each consume 12 kilos of avocados annually. It's a burden, but this recipe makes it bearable.

Ingredients

- ½ purple onion, diced
- 1-2 teaspoon wasabi powder, paste, or freshly grated root
- 1 teaspoon water (if using wasabi powder)
- 3 ripe avocados
- Grated zest and juice of 2 limes
- 1 tablespoon pickled ginger, minced
- 1 teaspoon sea salt
- ¼ cup cilantro leaves, minced
- 1 package square wonton wrappers
- Frying oil

Method

1. Cover the diced onion in cold water and set aside. This removes offending oils that cause your breath to stink. (The world appreciates this.) Stir together wasabi powder and water, and set aside for 15 minutes.

2. Halve and pit the avocados, scoop their meat into a large bowl, and mash with a fork. Stir in lime zest, juice, and pickled ginger. Add the salt, wasabi, and mix. Fold in onions and cilantro. Adjust seasoning, then cover with a sheet of plastic wrap pressed directly on the surface, which will prevent discoloration. Set aside at room temperature while you fry the chips.

3. Heat about 2 inches of oil in a heavy skillet to 375°F. When it reaches temperature, drop in 4-5 wonton skins (don't crowd them) and cook until golden brown, about 1 minute on each side. Remove to a paper towel lined tray, then sprinkle with salt. Repeat with remaining wonton wrappers. Serve guac with wonton wrappers and rice crackers. Now you are very hip.

Potato Skins Night Boogie
(Skin Tight Boogie, *Zipper Down*, 2015)

These **Loaded Potato Skins** were created for after-party nourishment. (The polite way to say "hangover food".) If you aren't hung over, they make a hearty breakfast. But we all know you are.

Ingredients

- 4 russet potatoes, baked in an oven or microwave
- 4 slices bacon, diced
- 1 large egg
- Pinch of sea salt and black pepper
- 1 cup grated cheddar cheese
- 1 tablespoon sour cream
- 1 ripe tomato, diced
- 2 scallions, chopped
- 1 avocado, diced
- 1 tablespoon chives or scallion greens, chopped

Method

1. Preheat oven to 375°F. Coat a baking sheet with pan spray. Slice the cooked potatoes into quarters lengthwise. Scoop out most of the white inner potato, leaving just a half-inch clinging to the skin. Set them skin-side-down on a baking sheet. *(Save the inner potato for future mashed potatoes. Not futuristic, like glow in the dark. Future, like tomorrow. By the way, I think "Future Mashed Potatoes" should be the name of our next favorite super-group.)*

2. Cook bacon in a small skillet over medium heat until the fat is rendered and the meat is crispy. Drain off all but 1 teaspoon of fat. Add the beaten egg, salt, pepper, and cook, stirring, until firm. Divide the egg evenly onto the top of each skin. Top each skin with diced tomato, green onion, and cheddar cheese. Bake for 5-10 minutes, until the cheese is melted and bubbly. Serve topped with avocado, sour cream, and chopped chives.

Main Stage

Entrees.　Sides.

Everyone needs to eat. You can be like most people, and just cram *whatever* into your mouth hole. Or you can be one of the cool kids. Turn the daily feed into a work of art.

Cooking is a lot like music. It can suck, or it can be a motherfucking sparkling rainbow unicorn of awesome. It can be artful, or it can be a cocksplatting piece of crap. It can be an international super-hit, or a Eurovision catastrophe. Your dinner doesn't have to be Michelin-starred to be worth a shit. Even a PB&J can be damn fine if it's made with fervor. (Side note: there's no recipe for a goddamn PB&J here.)

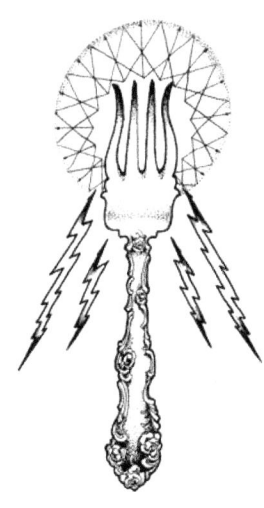

Baby Duck

Inspired by Joshua "Baby Duck" Homme,
co-founder of Eagles of Death Metal

This version of classic **Duck à l'Orange** is going to blow
your fucking mind. It combines waterfowl and hipster
citrus in a way no other chef has *dared* to in the history of this week. Waddle you do with the leftovers? Use
them in the *Salad of Queen Bee and Baby Duck*, page 6.

Ingredients

- 1 large carrot, roughly chopped
- 1 stalk celery, roughly chopped
- 1 small yellow onion, roughly chopped
- 1 5-6 pound whole duck - *Look for Peking, Musco-
  voy, or Magret ducks. If you have trouble finding
  duck, go to an Asian market, where no one is
  afraid to eat Daffy.*
- Sea salt and pepper to taste
- 1 cup water
- 1 tablespoon olive oil
- 1 leek, chopped
- 2 cloves garlic, chopped
- 2 bay leaves
- 1 teaspoon dried thyme
- 3 tablespoons all-purpose flour
- 1 cup white wine
- 2 cups chicken broth
- 5 blood oranges, tangerines, or other citrus
- 2 tablespoons cider vinegar
- 2 tablespoons Grand Marnier
- 2 tablespoons unsalted butter

Method

1. Preheat the oven to 450°F. Line the bottom of a
roasting pan with half the chopped carrot, celery, and
onions, creating a bed to set the bird on. Remove giblets from the duck cavity and set aside. Chop off the
wing tips and set aside with the giblets. (The wing tips
will burn in the oven). Prick the duck skin all over
with the tip of a sharp knife (*this helps the fat ren-
der*) then set the bird, tits up, into the pan and season
with salt and pepper. Place in the oven and roast, for
30 minutes, then turn the temperature down and continue

roasting for another 30-45 minutes, until the skin is golden and crispy, and the internal temperature, taken in the thickest spot of the thigh, reaches 165°F. (Coincidentally, that's where I prefer to have my temperature taken.)

2. Meanwhile, prepare the sauce. Heat the oil in a large saucepan, and add the giblets and wing tips. Cook over medium heat until browned, about 5 minutes. Add the remaining carrot, celery, and onion. Add the leeks, thyme, bay, and cook, stirring, until the vegetables are soft and translucent. Stir in the flour until all is well coated. Slowly add the wine and broth, stirring, to reach a sauce consistency. Bring to a boil, reduce to a simmer, and cook slowly for about an hour. After an hour, strain off all the liquid into a large bowl, and discard the solids.

3. Using a microplane, grate the zest off the blood oranges. Slice three zested oranges in half and squeeze the juice (you'll need at least 1 cup).

With a sharp knife, slice the top and bottom off the remaining zested oranges so they stand up straight. Slice from the top of the fruit to the bottom, removing the rind and the pith all the way around the fruit. The brightly colored inner fruit should now be exposed. Hold the fruit in your hand and slice to the center on each side of the membrane dividing each section. As you do this, the naked sections (aka *supremes*) will fall out. Do this over a bowl to catch extra juice. Squeeze all the juice you can out of the membrane, then discard the membrane. Boom! You just learned a classic culinary technique. You're welcome.

4. Combine the sugar and vinegar in a small saucepan and cook over high heat until it begins to caramelize (about 3-5 minutes). Carefully add the orange juice and zest, and bring to a boil. Add the strained duck sauce, bring to a simmer and cook for about 10 minutes. Remove from the heat, season with salt and pepper, then stir in Grand Marnier and butter.

5. Carve the roasted duck into serving pieces (2 breasts, 2 wings, 2 leg and thighs), and arrange them on a platter. Garnish with blood orange supremes and a thin drizzle of sauce. Pass the remaining sauce separately. Serve with a light green salad and a plucky swagger.

So Cheesy
(So Easy, Peace, Love, Death Metal, 2004)

Macaroni and Cheese is generally thought of as "comfort food", a fucking annoying phoodie term. Translated into plain-speak, comfort foods are fattening, high carb, nap-inducing foods you turn to for secret-feeling-eating. Just because this recipe is festooned with **lobster**, and you could conceivably serve it on a white tablecloth, doesn't mean you can't also eat it in your bunny slippers. Anyway, lobster isn't all that. In the 19th and early 20th Centuries, these crustaceans were so plentiful that they were routinely used as bait for more desirable fish. The ultimate sacrifice, which causes us to question the stereotype of lobster shellfishness.

Ingredients

- 1 lobster tail
- 1 tablespoon olive oil
- 1 pound macaroni noodles- *or shells, bowties, ziti - anything short and fat*
- 4 tablespoons unsalted butter
- ½ yellow onion, diced
- 1 stalk celery, diced
- 1 clove garlic, minced
- 3 tablespoon all-purpose flour
- 2 cups milk
- Sea salt and pepper to taste
- 1 pound Italian fontina, gouda, or muenster cheese, grated
- 2 cups crushed Ritz cracker crumbs
- 2 tablespoons grated parmesan cheese
- 1 tablespoon herbes de Provence, or dried thyme

Method

1. Preheat broiler. Cut open the length of the top of the lobster shell with kitchen shears. Drizzle it lightly with olive oil, place it on a baking sheet, and broil it for 5-10 minutes, until the meat is opaque and the shells are browned. Cool until they can be handled, then remove the tail meat and cut it into bite-sized

chunks and set it aside. (You can also do this on a grill.)

2. Bring a large pot of water to a boil. Add the macaroni and stir, bringing it back to the boil. Cook for 5-10 minutes, until the noodles are half-cooked. Strain off the water, cover the pasta with cold water to stop the cooking, and set aside.

3. Preheat the oven to 350° F. Melt 3 tablespoons of butter in a large saucepan over medium-high heat. Add the onions, celery, garlic, and cook, stirring, until the vegetables are tender and translucent. Add the flour and stir until all is well coated, then cook another minute until the flour begins to brown. Add the milk slowly, stirring out any lumps as you go. Cook until the sauce is thick, then transfer to a large baking dish. Season the sauce with salt and pepper, then add the cheese and stir until mostly melted. Add the lobster and macaroni, stir until well coated, and spread evenly in the baking dish. Mix the cracker crumbs with parmesan, herbes, and sprinkle it on top of the dish. Dot the top with remaining butter, then bake until golden brown, about 20 minutes. Serve warm. It's clawfully good.

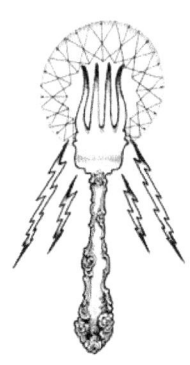

San Berdoo Sunchokes

(San Berdoo Sunburn, *Peace Love Death Metal*, 2004)

San Berdoo is the vernacular for San Bernardino, a city about halfway between the desert and LA. Sunchokes, also known as Jerusalem Artichokes, are crazy-looking tubers with a flavor similar to artichokes. This easy recipe for **Crispy Sunchokes with Rosemary and Balsamic** is lip-smacking good, unless you don't like regular artichokes, in which case you are going to fucking hate this recipe. If that's you, just move along. That'll leave more for the rest of us.

Ingredients

- 3 tablespoons olive oil
- 3 pounds small sunchokes, washed and cut into bite-sized chunks
- 2-3 springs fresh rosemary
- 2 bay leaves
- 1 teaspoon sea salt
- 4-5 tablespoons unsalted butter
- ¼ cup sliced almonds
- ¼ cup balsamic vinegar

Method

1. Heat olive oil in a large sauté pan over medium-high heat. Add the Jerusalem artichokes and cook, stirring, until they begin to brown. Add wine, water, and reduce to a simmer. Cover and cook about 10 minutes, until tender.

2. Remove cover from pan and increase heat. Cook, stirring occasionally, until all the liquid is evaporated, and the sunchokes are crispy, another 5-10 minutes. Remove from the pan and set aside.

3. Combine rosemary, bay, and salt in a coffee mill or mortar, then grind into a fine powder. In the same pan add the butter, ground herbs, almonds, and cook until the butter begins to brown. Remove from heat, add the vinegar and stir until smooth. Add the Jerusalem artichokes back in and toss until well coated. Serve warm or at room temperature. You're gunna love this dish, and that's no choke.

Speaking in Beef Tongue Tacos
(Speaking in Tongues, *Peace Love Death Metal,* 2004)

Finally! A dinner that tastes *you.* If you are a cool, groovy, with-it hep cat, then you are either a time traveling beatnik from 1952, or you have the kind of discriminating taste that will appreciate a dish like this one. Hipster-dufus cred aside, beef tongue is an incredibly meaty organ. (BTW, Meaty Organ was the name of my burlesque accordion band.) This dish, **Tacos de Lengua**, is what those in the first world might call "peasant food." But a well-prepared tongue is epicurean delight, so don't be a snooty twonk.

Ingredients

- 1 2-3 pound beef tongue—*there are other tongues you can use, but beef is most readily available. FYI, walrus tongue is particularly delicious — "coo coo cachew"*
- 1 tablespoon black peppercorns
- 3 bay leaves
- 2 large dried chiles, chopped roughly (I like to use pasilla or guajillo chiles)
- 1 onion, chopped roughly
- 1 stalk celery, chopped
- 1 carrot, chopped
- 3 cloves garlic, skinned and chopped
- 1 purple onion, diced
- 1-2 jalapeño peppers, diced
- 2 tomatoes, diced,
- ¼ cup cilantro, chopped
- 3-4 radishes, chopped
- 2 cups shredded cabbage
- 1 avocado, diced
- ½ cup crema or sour cream
- 10-12 corn tortillas (*2 per taco*)

1. Wash tongue thoroughly and soak in cold water for 1 hour. Change the water and soak again for another hour.

2. Fill a large pot with cold water. Add peppercorns, bay, chiles, onion, celery, carrot and garlic, and set

over high heat. At the boil, add the tongue. Be sure it is submerged. Reduce the heat to a simmer, cover, and cook slowly, for about 3 hours—about 1 hour per pound. (*This is important — if the heat is to high the tongue will toughen. Only fuck trumpets like their tongue tough.*) Add more water as necessary to keep the tongue submerged.

3. When ready, the tongue will be white, and a knife will enter easily into the thickest portion. Remove the tongue and cool slightly. While the tongue is still warm, peel off the outer white layer. (This is much easier to do when warm. Use tongs if necessary. If it cools too much, submerging it in cold water helps. Slice the tongue meat thinly, on the bias.

4. Heat oil in a large skillet over high heat. Add slices of the tongue meat and fry until extra crispy on each side. (*You can do this on a grill too, which is char-a-licious.*) Work in batches, careful not to overcrowd the pan. Remove the fried meat to a side platter and reserve. When all the meat is fried, add onion, jalapeno, and garlic to the same pan and cook until caramelized. Add tomatoes, lime, and cumin. Stir to combine, season with salt and pepper, then remove from heat and toss with the meat. Keep warm.

5. Toss together the cabbage, radish and cilantro. Warm the tortillas. To assemble the tacos, start with a base of two tortillas. Add a pinch of tongue meat, a small pile of slaw, a slice of avocado and a drizzle of crema. Now aren't you glad you put a little tongue in your taco?

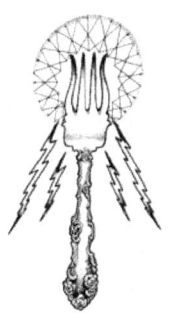

Midnight Leaper
(Midnight Creeper, *Peace Love Death Metal,* 2004)

I like Kermit as much as the next guy. But fuck it. These **Cajun Fried Frogs Legs** are delicious. Historically a French dish (why do you think they call the French "Frogs"?), the consumption of frog legs became a Cajun tradition, because wild bullfrogs are predatory pests to crayfish farmers. Bull Frogs can eat their weight in crayfish every few days, and they get ginormous. Rayne, Louisiana celebrates them at an annual festival in May, where, unlike the pansy-ass jumping frog races of Calaveras County, it's about feed, not speed.

Ingredients

For the Legs:
- 2 cups buttermilk
- ⅓ cup Tabasco
- ⅓ cup Cajun seasoning
- 1 tablespoon garlic powder
- 1 tablespoon onion powder
- 1 tablespoon good Hungarian paprika
- 1 teaspoon black pepper
- 12 individual frogs legs
- 2 cups all-purpose flour
- 1 teaspoon sea salt
- Frying oil

For the Mustard Creole Cream:
- 1 tablespoon olive oil
- 1 tablespoon unsalted butter
- 2 shallots, minced
- 2 cloves garlic, minced
- 1 teaspoon dried thyme
- Grated zest and juice of 1 lemon
- ¼ cup Italian parsley leaves, chopped
- 1 cup heavy cream
- ½ cup Dijon mustard
- ¼ teaspoon capers
- ¼ teaspoon gherkins or cornichons, minced
- Tabasco to taste
- Sea salt and pepper to taste

Method

1. Combine the buttermilk and Tabasco. Mix the Cajun seasoning, garlic and onion powders, paprika, and pepper in a small bowl. Add half of this mixture to the buttermilk. Add the legs, coat well, and refrigerate for at least 2 hours. (Overnight is better if possible.)

2. Meanwhile, make the Mustard Creole Cream. Heat oil and butter in a large sauté pan over medium-high heat. Add the shallots, garlic, and thyme. Cook, stirring, until tender and translucent. Add the lemon zest and juice, parsley, and cream. Let the cream bubble and reduce by half. Remove from heat and stir in the mustard, capers, gherkins, and Tabasco. Season and set aside, keeping warm until service.

4. Strain legs out of buttermilk, and let sit in a colander for a few minutes to dry. Mix remaining spices with flour, then add the legs and toss to coat thoroughly.

5. Heat 2-3 inches of oil in a large, heavy bottomed skillet. When the temperature reaches 350° F add a batch of legs. Don't crowd them in the pan. When golden brown on all sides, remove to a paper towel-lined platter and keep warm. Repeat with remaining legs. Sprinkle with salt, and serve hot with a dipping dish of Mustard Creole Cream—and a diet croak.

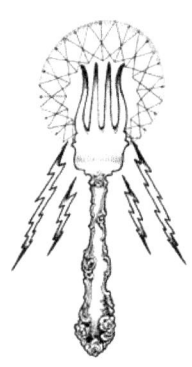

Don't Leek, I Came to Make Banger
(Don't Speak (I came to Make a Bang), *Death by Sexy*, 2006)

"Banger" is certainly the most inspired name for a wiener ever. It comes not from indiscrete use by *the ladies*, but from their habit of popping (or making a bang) as they cook. This recipe for **Homemade English Bangers with Leeks, Garlic, and Onions** is a sexy labor of love—just like bangin'. And like bangin', stuffing sausage isn't all that difficult. Just take your time, and try to enjoy it. Practice makes perfect.

Ingredients

- 15-20 feet of hog casings
- 4 pounds pork shoulder, cut into chunks, well chilled
- 1 pound pork fat, cut into chunks, well chilled
- 2½ tablespoons sea salt
- 1 tablespoon white pepper
- 1 tablespoon dried sage
- 1 teaspoon onion powder
- 1 teaspoon freshly grated nutmeg
- 8 ounces oatmeal, ground fine *(do this in a food processor, coffee mill, or mortar)*
- ¼ cup beer — your choice. If you're willing to drink it, you should be willing to cook with it
- 2 large yellow onions, sliced
- 2 large leeks, sliced *(just the white and very light green parts)* and well washed
- 4 scallions, chopped *(use white and green parts)*
- 4 cloves garlic, minced
- 1 cup white wine
- Salt and pepper to taste

Method

1. Soak the hog casings in warm water. Chill the grinder blades, bowl, meat, and fat for at least 60 minutes.

2. Mix the chilled meat and fat with salt, pepper, sage, onion powder, and nutmeg. Grind them through a coarse plate (10mm). Chill again for 30 minutes, then pass through a fine plate (4-5mm). Place the ground meat in

the freezer for another 30 minutes, until it reaches 32°F.

3. Mix the well-chilled ground and seasoned meat with the oats and beer. You may need to use your hands to really mix it thoroughly.

4. Stuff meat into hog casings loosely. You can do this manually, with a funnel, or with a mechanical stuffer. (*Many standing mixers have a grinding and stuffing attachment*). Twist into links that are about 6 inches long. If you see air pockets, pierce through the casings with a sterilized pin, and press the air out. Place your wieners on a tray and rest them in the refrigerator for several hours, or overnight.

5. Preheat the oven to 375° F. Heat butter in a large skillet over medium-high heat. Add 6-8 sausages and cook, rotating, to brown on all sides. (Don't worry if they are cooked through at this point). Remove from the pan and reserve. In the same skillet, add the onion and leeks. Cook, stirring, until tender and translucent. Add the scallions and garlic, and cook another minute. Stir in the wine, salt pepper, then place the browned bangers on top. Place the skillet in the oven and roast for 30 minutes, until the bangers begin to burst. Serve your wieners and leeks with a wink and a nudge.

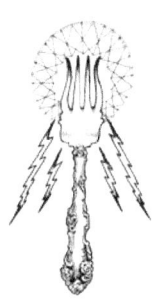

Solid Mold
(Solid Gold, *Death by Sexy*, 2006)

Blue cheese is mold. That's just science. But it's delightful mold. And with it, you can make these delicious
Potato Gorgonzola Gnocchi. Gnocchi are kick-ass dough
wads. The love child of pasta and dumplings. They come
in many incarnations, from many regions of Italy. But
this one is the best, because potato. Gorgonzola is a
blue cheese from Milan. It's made by introducing spores
of *Penicillium glaucum*. (Just calm the fuck down. All
blue cheese is made this way.) In the old days (like 900
AD) gorgonzola was stored in cool, moist caves that nat-
urally contained perfectly safe and delightful molds
that made the cheese tangy, salty, and creamy. (Like a
good man.) These days the mold is added by the cheese
maker. Metal spikes are jabbed into the cheese, creating
channels of air that encourage the mold to grow. It's
these jabby spore channels that make gorgonzola a-
fucking-mazing. Also, the Jabby Spore Channel is where
you can find the best late night Sci-Fi porn.

Ingredients

- 2 pounds russet potatoes, peeled and halved
- ½ teaspoon sea salt
- 1 ½ cup all-purpose flour
- ½ pound gorgonzola
- 3 tablespoons unsalted butter
- ½ cup heavy cream
- ¼ cup freshly grated parmesan cheese

Method

1. Place potatoes in a large pot, cover with cold water,
and bring to a boil over high heat. Cook until tender,
then drain. Pass the cooked potatoes through a ricer or
a wire mesh strainer into a bowl, then let cool.

2. Add the salt, then slowly stir in the flour until the
mixture becomes a dough. Divide into four pieces, and
roll each into a log about an inch thick. Cut 1-inch
pieces off the logs, then press and roll each piece over
a gnocchi board, or the back of a fork. This creates
ridges that will cling to the sauce later. Rest the
formed gnocchi in a single layer on a tray dusted with
flour.

3. Melt butter in a large skillet over medium heat. Let it brown, then add gorgonzola and stir to melt. Stir in the cream and pepper. Turn to low heat and keep warm.

4. Meanwhile, bring a pot of salted water to a boil. Drop the gnocchi into the boiling water in batches. When they rise to the surface, remove them with a slotted spoon, and add to the gorgonzola sauce. Repeat with remaining gnocchi. Toss to coat, then serve, sprinkled with parmesan, and prepare to be adored, because this dish is grate.

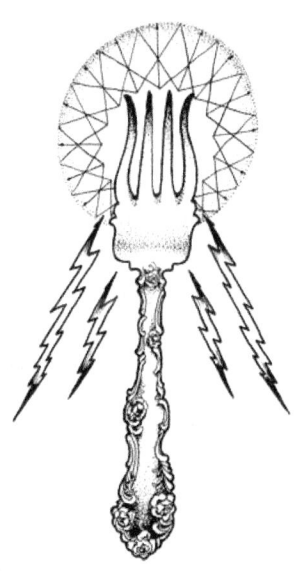

I Got a Peeling
(I Got a Feeling, *Death by Sexy,* 2006)

Plantains are the banana's exotic cousin. Less sweet and more starchy, dishes like **Fried Plantains** are standard fare in Caribbean and Latin American cuisines. Served with a hotsy-totsy dipping sauce, this recipe is an easy, fast way to get that nana goodness into your face. When choosing your plantains, remember that, when ripe, plantains are big, black, and hard. The blacker, the better. Like *Shaft*. (Who's the black private dick that's a sex machine to all the chicks? *Plantain!*)

Ingredients

For Dipping Sauce:
- ¼ cup olive oil
- ½ large red onion, minced
- 1 small red or yellow chile pepper, minced - try serrano or habanero *(Be careful! Use gloves! Don't rub your eye! Or your wiener!)*
- 2 cloves garlic, minced
- 1 teaspoon fresh oregano, chopped
- 1 teaspoon fresh thyme, chopped
- ½ teaspoon ground cumin
- ¼ teaspoon fresh cracked pepper
- Grated zest and juice of 1 lime
- 1 cup orange juice
- Sea salt, to taste

For Plantains:
- 4 ripe plantains
- 2 teaspoons sea salt
- ½ - 1 cup peanut or vegetable oil

Method

1. For the dipping sauce, heat a large sauté pan over medium heat. Add oil, then onion, chile, and cook until tender and translucent, about 30 seconds. Add garlic, oregano, thyme, cumin, and pepper. Cook another 30 seconds, then remove from heat. Stir in lime zest and juice, and orange juice. Season with salt as needed, then set aside to macerate at room temperature (*chef speak for letting it sit for a while*).

2. Slice the plantains about ½-inch thick, on the bias (*little ovals, instead of little circles*). Combine them in a bowl and toss with salt.

3. Preheat ¼ inch of oil in a large sauté pan over high heat. Add a handful of plantain slices when the oil is hot. (*It should be about 375°F, but you don't need a thermometer- just add a bit of plantain and see if it bubbles. If not, let it heat a little longer.*) Fry until golden and crispy, about 1-2 minutes on each side. Work in batches so as not to crowd the pan, which would prevent browning. When done, remove from the pan with a slotted spoon and transfer to a paper towel to drain. Repeat with the rest of the plantains. Serve hot with the dipping sauce. They are also amazing with a bowl of black beans, beans (*the musical fruit*). Top it with a dollop of sour cream and a little chopped cilantro, then strut right out into the dining room like a goddamn peacock. Now you're a bad mother (shut your mouth)!

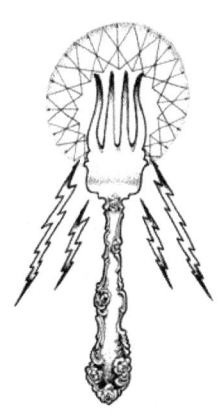

Porkchoppin' (Shit, Goddamn, That's Good)
(Whorehoppin'(Shit, Goddamn), *Death by Sexy*, 2006)

You will be a motherfuckin' rock star when you make this recipe. These **Thick-Cut Pork Chops, Stuffed with Apples, Fennel, and Sage** definitely take some effort, which will be obvious to your guests. That makes this the perfect recipe if you need to apologize, impress a client, or get laid. It's your go-to kiss-ass meal.

Ingredients

- 4 tablespoons unsalted butter, divided
- 1 bulb fennel, diced — *This is sometimes labeled "sweet anise" in the market.*
- 1 yellow onion, diced
- ¼ cup fresh sage, minced, plus a handful of whole leaves for garnish
- 2 apples, peeled and diced - *I prefer Fuji apples, but you can use whatever you like. But stay away from Granny Smith. That bitch. I hate her apples.*
- 1 clove garlic, minced
- 1 cup white wine
- ½ teaspoon sea salt
- ¼ teaspoon ground black pepper
- 4 thick-cut porch chops —*If you don't eat piggies, this recipe works great with lamb or veal chops, a venison steak, or even some cow. (See the Variations)*
- 2-4 tablespoons olive oil
- ¼ cup additional white wine
- Additional sea salt as needed

Method

1. Melt 2 tablespoons of butter in a large sauté pan over medium-high heat. Add fennel, onion, and minced sage. Cook, stirring, until translucent. Add apples, garlic, and cook another 2-3 minutes, stirring, until garlic is fragrant, and everything starts to caramelize. Stir in white wine and scrape all the good stuff off the bottom of the pan. Reduce heat to medium-low, and cook until the apples are tender and the liquid is evaporated, about 5 minutes. Remove from heat, season, and cool completely. (*To cool it quick, spread onto a baking sheet in a thin layer and throw it in the freezer.*)

2. Using a sharp knife (*A boning knife works well for this, because the tip is thin …which sounds like a personal problem. BTW, in the biz we call the boning knife "The Boner"… because chefs are cool like that.*) Slice a pocket into the thick side of the chop, on the opposite side from the bone. Make the cavity as large as you can, but try to keep the opening as small as you can. The goal is to pack as much stuffing into the hole as possible. This is also, I'm fairly certain, the goal of every hot-blooded male.

3. When the stuffing is totally cool, use a spoon (or your hands, which is, frankly, much easier) and fill each cavity. If it appears your stuffing will spill out easily, seal it with a toothpick.

4. Preheat the oven to 375°F. Heat the sauté pan again and add the oil. Sear the stuffed chops on each side, until well charred. Season with a little salt and pepper, then transfer to a baking dish and cook in the oven for 30-40 minutes, until the internal temperature is 145°F. Take them out of the oven and let them rest for 5 minutes.

5. Meanwhile, in the same sauté pan, fry sage leaves in a little olive oil for a crispy, classy garnish. Then, also in the same pan, make a quick sauce by melting the butter and cooking until it starts to brown. Add the wine and bring to a boil, scraping up all the tasty bits off the bottom of the pan. (By the way, when I write for Harlequin, "Tasty Bits" is my *nom de plume*.) Season with salt and pepper, and pour over your chop. Garnish with your pretty fried sage leaf and serve. Then prepare to get laid because this dish is just that good.

Variations:
If you'd like to use this with gamier meats (Lamb, Venison) consider switching from apples to pears. The flavor is a little sweeter, and thus, a little more complimentary. With beef I really prefer a stronger stuffing, and will often add an ounce or two of Gorgonzola or other good blue cheese to the cooled apple mixture. Don't try to look for beef chops. They will be Flintstone-sized. Just use a thick cut steak. Yabba Dabba Do.

Secret Yams (aka "Roots Electric")
(Secret Plans, *Heart On*, 2008)

This dish of warm **roasted root vegetables** can be served hot, as a side dish, or room temperature, as a salad. Before you begin, you should know that the orangey root vegetable you've been eating all your life is actually not a yam. The thing your Aunt Effie brings to Thanksgiving every year slathered in brown sugar is a sweet potato. I know Effie calls it "candied yams," but Effie is an effin' amateur.

Real yams have white or purple flesh, a thick scaly skin, and are extremely starchy and sweet. Your market carries orange and yellow varieties of sweet potatoes, which are botanically unrelated to a true yam. Modern grocers decided to call the orange potato *"Yam"* to distinguish it from the yellow. Smooth move Ex-Lax. Now no one knows what the fuck's going on with tubers in America. (BTW, Candied Yams is the name I used to dance under.)

Ingredients

- 1 yam or sweet potato — *whatever your grocer calls it. By the way, I bet he'd love it if you set him straight. You should totally explain the yam thing to him.*
- 1 butternut squash
- 1 red or yellow beet — *Be aware that the red ones stain everything they touch once cut. Keep them segregated on the cutting board and in the pan.*
- 1 parsnip — *If you don't know what a parsnip is, try reading the grocery store signage, you fucking twonk. It looks like a fat white carrot.*
- 1 yellow onion
- 1-2 tablespoons olive oil
- 1 teaspoon sea salt
- ½ teaspoon fresh cracked black pepper
- 2 slices of bacon, chopped — *if you're a vegetarian you can use another tablespoon of olive oil here*
- 2 cloves garlic, sliced
- 1 tablespoon honey
- 1 tablespoon cider vinegar
- 1 cup apple juice

- ½ cup pomegranate seeds
- ½ cup toasted pecans, chopped
- ¼ cup crumbled feta or goat cheese

Method

1. Preheat oven to 375°F. Peel and dice the squash, potato, beet, and parsnip, into 1-2 inch chunks. Quarter the onion, leaving the root in tact. Toss them all in olive oil and spread them out onto a baking sheet. Roast until they are tender and charred on the outside, about 30-45 minutes. Sprinkle with ½ teaspoon of salt and the black pepper, then set aside at room temperature.

2. Meanwhile cook the bacon in a large sauté pan over medium heat, until it is crisp and the fat is rendered, about 1-2 minutes. Add the garlic and cook until translucent, about 30-60 seconds. Stir in honey, vinegar, and apple juice. Bring to a boil and cook, stirring, until the liquid is reduced to syrupy, glazy consistency, about 3-5 minutes. Keep your eye on this. It will happen fast!

3. Combine the glaze, roasted roots, pecans, and pomegranate seeds in a large bowl and toss to coat. Season with more salt as needed, top with crumbled cheese, and serve with pride, like the sweet potato laureate you are.

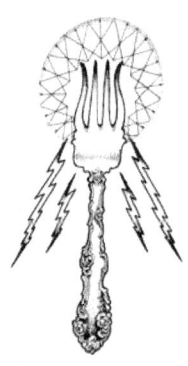

I'm your Tournedo
(I'm Your Tornado, *Heart On,* 2008)

A **Tournedo** is the classic French preparation of beef tenderloin, created for composer Gioachino Rossini (Barber of Seville, William Tell Overture, etc … not that you clueless numpties would get that reference) who was the Mick Jagger of his day. He was a hugely famous, wildly popular, extremely rich, gloriously demanding, and a total dick. When the menu wasn't to his liking, he demanded that special dishes be created for him. Waiters were said to have turned their backs (*tourner le dos*) as they entered the dining room with his special orders, so no other guest would see and want it. That story should be motivation enough to make this recipe. Who gives a fuck what's in it? It's so goddamn awesome that it has to be hidden from the masses. It's the culinary equivalent of whatever's inside Marsellus Wallace's glowing briefcase.

Ingredients

- 2 tablespoons butter
- 4 thin slices best French bread
- 4 3-4 ounce beef tenderloin medallions
- Sea salt and pepper to taste
- 4 strips extra-thick bacon
- 4 slices foie gras or liver pâté
- 1 shallot, minced
- 1 sprig fresh thyme
- ¼ cup red wine or madeira
- 1 tablespoon veal demiglace - *Available at a schmancy grocery store- usually in the freezer section. You can make your own by reducing a good stock to a syrup consistency.*

Method

1. Melt 1 tablespoon of the butter in a large skillet. Add the French bread slices and quickly fry until toasted on each side, 1-2 minutes. Remove from heat and reserve.

2. Season the beef medallions with salt and pepper on both sides. Wrap one bacon strip around the circumference of each and secure with a toothpick.

3. Place the same skillet over high heat. Put the medallions in the pan, bacon edge down, and cook until the bacon
i
s well charred. (There will, and should, be smoke. Turn on the vent and open a window.) Rotate the medallions to char the bacon on all sides. Place the flat beef sides down and sear about 2-3 minutes on each side for medium rare. Remove from the heat and keep warm. In the same pan, lightly fry foie gras to warm through, about 90 seconds per side. Place one fried foie on top of each filet.

4. In the same pan melt remaining butter over medium high heat. Add shallots and cook until lightly golden. Add thyme, wine, and cook to reduce liquid by half. Stir, scraping the bottom of the pan while you reduce, to release all the good crusty bits on the bottom. Remove from heat, season to taste, then strain.

5. To serve, place toasted crouton on the plate. Remove toothpicks from tournedos and set each foie-topped medallion on top of each crouton. Drizzle lightly with sauce. You can top it with shaved truffle a la Rossini, if you're like that. Serve with some dainty veg, like asparagus, or steamed baby carrots, because you're a posh motherfucker.

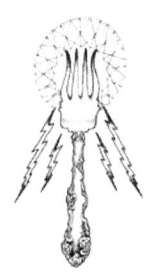

Anything Cèpes the Truth
(Anything 'Cept the Truth, *Heart On*, 2008)

This Wild Mushroom Risotto recipe uses French Cèpes,
which are wild mushrooms (*Boletus Edulis*). They are also
known as *porcini* in Italy, and *Penny Bun* in England. And
if you're wondering why cèpes grow so close together,
it's because they don't need mushroom.

Ingredients

* 1 ounce dried cèpes/porcini, or shitaki mushrooms
* ½ pound fresh button or crimini mushrooms (*crimini are baby portobellos*)
* 4 cups beef, chicken, or vegetable stock
* 4 tablespoons unsalted butter
* 4 ounces pancetta or bacon, diced
* 2 large shallots or ½ yellow onion
* 1½ cup Arborio rice (*This rice has short, fat grains, and is very starchy*)
* ½ cup white wine
* ½ teaspoon sea salt, plus more to taste
* ½ teaspoon black pepper
* ½ cup freshly grated parmesan cheese
* ¼ cup chopped Italian parsley

Method

1. Cover dried mushrooms with warm water and set aside
for about 30 minutes. When soft, remove from the water,
pat dry, and dice. Pour the mushroom water into a large
saucepan with the chicken stock. Bring to a boil, reduce
to low heat, then keep warm on a back burner.

2. Heat a large skillet, add the butter, pancetta, and
shallots. Sauté, stirring, until translucent. Add dried
and fresh mushroom, and the rice. Sauté, stirring, until
the rice is well coated with fat and the mushrooms begin
to soften. Add the wine and cook until the liquid is reduced.

3. Add salt and pepper, and ½ cup of stock. Stir until
the liquid is absorbed, then add another ½ cup of stock.
Stir and cook slowly again. Repeat this process until
all the stock is absorbed. It will take about 30
minutes. The slow additions and continuous stirring
gives risotto its creamy texture. The rice should be

tender, creamy, and thick, but not mushy (*al dente* is
the term often used to describe this, though only by
bloviating fleshbags that fancy themselves "chefs").
Stir in parmesan cheese and serve, topped with parsley
and a little more parm, if you like. And you *will*
like.

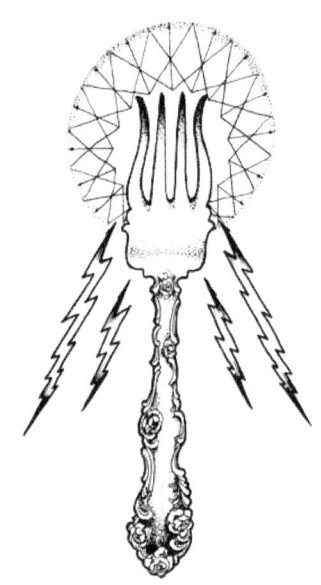

Pie Voltage
(High Voltage, *Heart On,* 2008)

This is the **Chicken Potpie** of the rock gods. If you have
only ever had Swanson's frozen potpie, you are in for a
goddamn confetti shower of wonderfullness. You will be
dumbfounded at the way ordinary ingredients become ex-
traordinary. Like all great cooking, it's a little bit
magical.

Ingredients

- 4 tablespoons unsalted butter
- ½ yellow onion, diced
- 1 stalk celery, diced
- 1 large carrot, diced
- 4 small red potatoes, diced
- ½ cup white wine
- ½ cup water
- 1 tablespoon dried herbes de Provence, or dried
  thyme
- ½ teaspoon freshly grated nutmeg
- ¼ cup all-purpose flour
- 1½ cup milk
- ½ teaspoon sea salt, plus more to taste
- ½ teaspoon black pepper
- 2 cups cooked chicken meat, shredded or diced.
  (*Next time you make chicken, make some extra for
  use in this recipe*)
- 1 cup fresh or frozen peas
- 1 cup grated white or yellow cheddar cheese
- 1 9-inch circle of pie dough or puff pastry,
  rolled to ¼ inch thick
- 1 egg yolk
- 1 teaspoon heavy cream
- 2 tablespoons grated parmesan cheese

Method

1. Melt butter in a large sauté pan over medium high
heat. Add onion, celery, carrot, and potato. Cook, stirring, until tender and translucent. Add wine and water,
bring to a boil, then reduce to a simmer and cook, covered for 10 minutes, until potatoes are tender. Remove

lid and continue to cook on high to reduce all the liquid.

2. Add thyme, nutmeg, and flour, and stir until well coated. Slowly add the milk, a little at a time, stirring continuously to work out any lumps. When all the milk is in, add salt and pepper to taste, and remove from the heat. (*For those of you keeping score, this is essentially a classic béchamel sauce.*)

3. Preheat oven to 350° F. Off the heat stir in the chicken and peas. Transfer to an 8-inch pie pan or similar baking dish, then top with cheese. Place pastry sheet on top, trim the edges, and crimp to fit. Prick the top with a knife to create a small vent. Mix together egg and cream, brush it on the top of the pastry, then sprinkle with parmesan cheese. Bake for 30-45 minutes, until the pastry is golden brown and the filling is bubbling through the vents. Cool slightly before serving. Now you are Lord of the Pies.

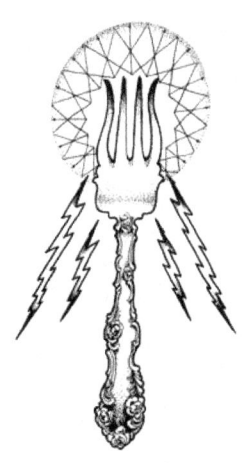

Silversteak
(K.C.O.F.M. "King Chef of Food Mountain")
(Silverlake (K.S.O.F.M.), *Zipper Down*, 2015)

This dish of **Pan-Fried Trout with Meyer Lemons, Almonds, and Capers** is readily available in Silverlake, a hipster enclave of LA, now immortalized in song. To be honest, the neighborhood isn't all that. This trout, however, is all that and more. Or, as James Beard use to say, "It's the tits!"

Ingredients

- 2 large Meyer lemons, regular lemons, or limes
- ½ large purple onion, minced
- ½ cup fresh Italian parsley, minced
- ½ cup fresh tarragon or basil leaves, minced
- 1 tablespoon capers
- 1 teaspoon sea salt
- 1 teaspoon Dijon mustard
- 2 tablespoons olive oil, divided
- 2 whole trout, cleaned and gutted *(keep skin on, and the head if you dare)*
- ½ teaspoon freshly cracked black pepper
- 2 tablespoons unsalted butter
- ½ cup sliced almonds
- ¼ cup capers

Method

1. Finely grate the zest from the lemon, and combine it on a cutting board with the onion, parsley, tarragon, capers, and ½ teaspoon of the salt. Chop them together to create a dry paste, then set aside in a large bowl. Add the mustard and 1 tablespoon of the olive oil. Mix well and set aside at room temperature.

3. Season the filets with the remaining salt and pepper. Heat a cast iron (or very heavy) skillet over high heat. Add remaining oil and butter. As soon as the fat is hot, add the fish and cook until golden brown, about 3-4 minutes. Carefully flip the fish and cook another 3-4 minutes, or to desired doneness. Remove the fish from the pan and keep warm.

4. Add the almonds to the to the empty fish pan and
cook, stirring, for 1-2 minutes to toast them. Add the
herb and mustard mixture, and stir to warm through.
Serve each filet topped with a generous portion of pan
sauce. This dish is sure to be your new gill-ty pleas-
ure.

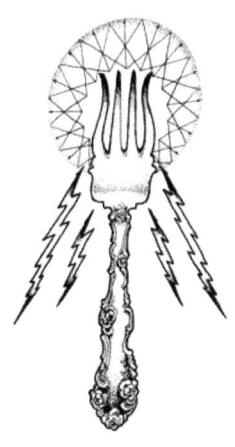

The Sweet Stuff

Desserts

Homemade dessert offers the most bang for your buck. In terms of culinary investment, it absolutely yields the highest return. Feeling lonely? You can make a lot of friends with a plate of cookies. Piss off your mate? A chocolaty cake presented with puppy dog eyes can get you out of the doghouse. A well-formed apple tart positioned strategically on your boss's desk is cause for promotion. And you can probably get backstage to see your favorite band with an artfully stacked tray of brownies and bars. I'm not making any promises, but if experience is any indicator, dessert wins.

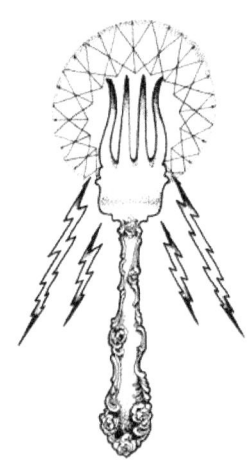

Cherry Cola Cake
(Cherry Cola, *Death by Sexy*, 2006)

The southern United States is obsessed with cola, probably because Coke is made there, and it gets hot as
balls. It is in this sweltering region that the **Cola
Cake** really took hold. A regular feature of church pot-
lucks and Civil War reenactments, this cake is more
popular than hair spray.

Cherry cola was popularized in the 19th century, when
cherry syrup was added to jazz up the medicinal flavor
of a carbonated beverage made with coca leaves and kola
nuts. It surged in popularity during prohibition, when
it was illegal to have a beer, but totally cool to suck
down a cocaine float.

This recipe is presented as a layer cake. But since you
are probably completely stoned, feel free to make it in
a rectangular brownie pan, which is faster.

Ingredients

- 2 cups fresh, frozen, or canned cherries, cleaned
  and pitted — *Avoid maraschino cherries, which have
  no actual cherry flavor or color. They are only
  good for demonstrations of tongue dexterity.*
- 2 teaspoons vanilla extract
- ¼ cup brandy or rum — *if you are on the wagon,
  this is optional*
- 1 cup unsalted butter, softened
- 1 ¾ cup granulated sugar
- 2 large eggs
- 2 cups all-purpose flour
- ¼ cup cocoa powder — *extra dark if possible*
- ½ teaspoon sea salt
- 1 teaspoon baking soda
- 1 cup cherry cola
- ½ cup buttermilk
- 1 cup mini chocolate chips or chunks
- 2 cups heavy whipping cream
- 2 tablespoons powdered sugar
- 1 chocolate bar for shaving

Method

1. Preheat oven to 350° F. Lightly coat two 8-inch round cake pans, or 1 brownie pan (9x13 inches) with pan spray. Chop the cherries and mix with vanilla and brandy, then set them aside.

2. Cream together butter and sugar until smooth and lump free. Lumps at this stage would suck. Add the eggs, one at a time, mixing well between each addition.

3. Sift together the flour, cocoa, baking soda, and salt. Separately combine the cherry cola and buttermilk. Add the dry and wet mixtures into the butter alternately, in about 3 increments, stirring well between each addition. *(This means add 1/3 of the flour, stir, then 1/3 of the buttermilk, stir, and repeat.)* Fold in chocolate and cherries, then pour the batter into the prepared pan. Bake for 30-45 minutes, until risen and firm. A toothpick inserted into the center should come out clean. Remove from oven and cool completely.

4. In a large bowl combine cream and sugar and whip until stiff. *(Do this by hand with a whisk if you're a stud, or use an electric mixer, if you skipped arm day at the gym.)* Spread the whipped cream evenly onto one layer. Then stack the layers and cover the top and sides with remaining cream. Use a potato peeler to shave curls off the chocolate bar to decorate. Keep chilled until you're ready to serve. You're gunna love this cherry much.

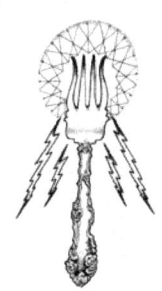

I Want Coo So Hard

(I Want You So Hard, *Death by Sexy*, 2006)

This is the World's Best Cookie recipe, and that's not hyperbole. It is fact. A team of scientists took part in a controlled study, comparing cookies from several different sources. The resulting score ranked this cookie higher in all variable fields, including type of chocolate, nuts, and flours.
Oh, wait.
They might not have been scientists. They might have been just a bunch of stoners.

Ingredients

- 1 cup unsalted butter.
- 1 cup granulated sugar
- 1 cup brown sugar — dark or light. As Bill Murray says in *Meatballs*, "it just doesn't matter."
- 1 tablespoon milk
- 1 tablespoon vanilla extract
- 2 large eggs
- 1 teaspoon baking soda
- ½ teaspoon baking powder
- 1 teaspoon sea salt
- 2 cup all-purpose flour
- 2 cups quick oats, uncooked
- 2 cups cornflakes — *not frosted flakes- that would not be grrrrreat*
- 1 cup chocolate chips
- ½ cup shredded coconut
- ½ cup pecan pieces

1. Preheat oven to 350° F. Coat a baking sheet with pan spray (or line it with parchment paper, like we do in the big leagues).

2. Beat together butter and sugars until smooth and lump free. One at a time, stir in milk, vanilla, and the eggs. Be sure each addition is well incorporated before the next goes in. Stir in baking soda, baking powder, salt, and finally the flour. Mix well. Fold in oats, cornflakes, chocolate chips, coconut and pecans. Now chill the dough for 10-20 minutes. *(At this point, you can also form it into logs and freeze it for several weeks!)*

3. Scoop walnut sized dough wads onto the prepared pan (or cut ½" thick discs off your frozen log) about an inch apart. Bake for 10 minutes, until firm and golden brown. Serve with a tall glass of milk so you can dunk 'em like Wilt the Stilt.

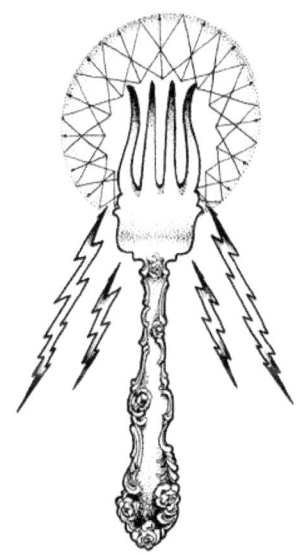

Tart On
(Heart On, *Heart On,* 2008)

This **Dark Chocolate Silk Tart** (Yeah, it's as good as it sounds) is a "for company" dish. It's the thing you make when you need to seal a deal. It takes some forethought. You'll need to dig in and concentrate. (Consider starting this recipe with a clear head.) I promise, it is definitely worth the extra effort.

The recipe is in two parts—the dough and the filling. The dough is the real skill, and once mastered, can be used to make any number of great desserts. Of course, you can cheat and buy a crust ready-made. But everyone will know you did that, and you'll probably be shunned. Don't say I didn't warn you.

Pâte Sucrée
(a sweet, buttery tart dough)

If baking is a rare occurrence in your kitchen, the dough for this tart shell is going to freak you the fuck out. But just go with the flow. I promise nothing bad will happen to you. The dough will crack if it's too cold, and it will stick if it's too warm. You'll need to calm down, and breathe. Too warm? Chill it. Too cold, let it sit on the counter a few minutes to warm up. Easy. My best advice is to work fast. Roll with purpose. Don't fiddle-fuck around answering the phone or whatever. Use plenty of flour on your worktable while rolling, and repeat to yourself, "Cooking is fun. Cooking is fun."

Ingredients

- 8 ounces unsalted butter (2 sticks)
- ½ cup granulated sugar
- 1 large egg
- 3 cups cake or all-purpose flour

Method

1. Cream together butter and sugar until smooth and lump-free. (You can do this in a standing mixer fitted with the paddle attachment, or by hand with a sturdy spoon like the stud I know you are.) Add the egg and beat until thoroughly combined. Add the flour all at once and stir it in slowly until a dough forms. (If you

don't do it slowly you'll get flour everywhere.) Divide it into two pieces, press them into flat discs, wrap in plastic, and chill. *(We do this because the dough needs to chill to be workable. But because this dough is half butter, it gets very hard in the fridge. The small flat packages are easier to work with. Who figured this out? A goddamn genius, that's who!)* Chill at least an hour. You can do this ahead of time, too. Professionals typically make dough in large batches, then freeze them in small packages for use throughout the week.

2. Coat a tart pan with pan spray. I suggest a false-bottom pan, which makes it easy to unmold and cut neatly. I also like tart rings, which basically form only the side of a pan. The parchment-lined baking sheet serves as the bottom. (By the way, Tart Rings is also the name of the nation's #1 selling blowjob lipstick remover.)

3. Dust your work surface with flour, and pinch off only as much dough as you'll need for one tart shell. (You will have to guesstimate this, which is a task I know you are fully capable of.) Knead it briefly to soften slightly, pat into a disc (start round, end round) and roll out to a circle a couple inches larger than your tart pan, and no more than ¼-inch thick.

There is a trick to this rolling business. Roll in one direction only, then give the dough ¼ turn after each roll. Roll, turn, roll, turn, until it is the size you need. This way, you will keep it roundish, and you will know instantly if it starts to stick, enabling you to compensate with a dusting of flour. If you press and roll the dough in one spot, it will surely stick, be uneven, look like shit, and frustrate you.

Line the tart pan, pressing the dough into place, and pinching off the top rim flush with the rim of the pan. If the dough cracks or tears, it is not a big deal. In fact, none of this is a big deal. It's just a tart, not a cure for cancer. Take a deep breath, and patch it as needed. When your shell is lined, freeze it for 10 minutes while you preheat your oven to 350°F.

4. Now it's time to blind-bake. We do this when the tart filling does not get cooked in the oven. The shell is filled with a fake filling to simulate the weight of a real filling, holding the dough in place as it bakes.

Take the dough shell out of the freezer, line it with foil, and fill it to the rim with dried beans or rice. (*Don't buy special pie weights or baking pearls or whatever the fuck they are trying to sell you. It's all a scam.*) Cook it until the rim begins to turn golden brown, about 20 minutes. Spin it around occasionally so that it browns evenly. When it looks to have solidified, very carefully remove the fake filling and liner, and return to the oven to bake until the bottom is golden brown and clearly cooked.

Remove the shell carefully from the oven and let it cool. At this point you could fill the shell with anything—pastry cream, chocolate mousse, salted caramel, fresh fruit—I'm sure you can come up with something amazing. Of course, for this recipe, you'll fill it with this:

Chocolate Silk Tart Filling

Ingredients

- 10 ounces dark bittersweet chocolate
- 3 ounces (¾ stick) unsalted butter
- ½ teaspoon sea salt
- ⅓ cup granulated sugar
- 1 teaspoon vanilla extract
- 3 large eggs
- ⅔ cup heavy cream

Method

1. Melt chocolate over a bain-marie. (*This is the French term for a double boiler. You can simply set a heatproof bowl over a pot of steaming, barely simmering water.*) Once completely melted keep the chocolate warm until you need it.

2. In a mixer, or by hand, cream together the butter, salt, and sugar until smooth and lump free. Add the vanilla, and the eggs, one at a time. The ratio of fat to liquid here is lopsided, and the mixture will look broken and wrong. Surprisingly, it's not you fault. That's how it is supposed to look. Just relax.

3. Add the still-warm melted chocolate and beat for 2 minutes. Add the cream last and beat briefly to combine.

Pour this chocolate silk filling into the cooled tart shell. Spread evenly, then chill for 1 hour. To serve, top with whipped cream, or fresh berries, powdered sugar, chocolate shavings, or anything else you think sounds good. If you are going to use cool whip #1, don't invite me, and #2, just be upfront about it, because everyone can tell the difference between that and an actual dairy product.

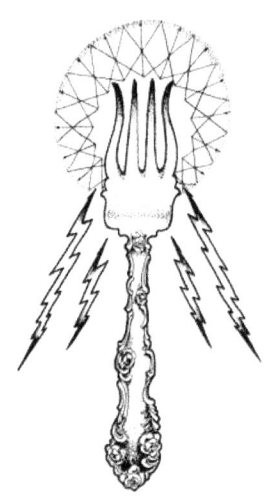

Pomme-Plexity
(Complexity, *Zipper Down*, 2015)

The best desserts are the simplest. This is as simple as
it gets. Except, wait, no. It's a bit tricky. **Le Tarte
Tatin** is the French apple tart that American apple pie
wishes it was. It is one of the classic pastry dishes
that chefs use to test potential employees. If you can
make this, you get the job. If not, hit the bricks.

Ingredients

- 6 oz. unsalted butter
- 1 ¾ cups sugar
- 6-8 large apples (Fuji apples are preferred)
- 1 sheet Puff pastry or pie dough - enough for a 9-
  inch circle, about ¼ inch thick

Method

1. Spread sugar evenly across the bottom
of an 8-inch heavy sauté pan. Cut the butter
into small chunks and distribute it evenly
across the sugar.

2. Peel, quarter, and core the apples.
Arrange them on top of the raw sugar and butter,
packed tightly, with cores facing the center of
the pan. Place the pan over medium heat and
cook until the sugar dissolves. Increase the
heat and cook until caramelized. Turn the pan
periodically to promote even cooking. When the
sugar is caramelized and thick, remove from the
heat and cool. Preheat oven to 400°F.

3. Cut a ¼-inch thick sheet of pastry into a circle 1
inch larger than the pan, and poke holes all over it
with a fork. (This keeps it from rising out of shape
while baking.) Place the pastry over the apples and the
tuck edges into pan.

4. Bake the pastry-topped pan of caramelized apples until the pastry is golden brown and the caramel is
bubbly, about 30-45 minutes. When done, remove from the
oven and let cool about 10 minutes. While still warm,
(but not scorching hot), invert onto a serving platter.
Serve warm with good French Vanilla ice cream.

Save a Layer ('till the Morning After)
(Save a Prayer, *Zipper Down,* 2015)

This is a guaranteed hit at any bake sale or smoke out.
Easier than cookies, less snooty than brownies, these
Eleven Layer Bars are fast and satisfying - like that
girl you met at Coachella. Why eleven layers? D'uh! Every cockwomble knows that in rock and roll we always turn
it up to eleven.

Ingredients

- 2 cups pretzels
- 2 cups graham crackers
- 2 tablespoon granulated sugar
- 1 stick melted butter
- 1 cup chocolate chips
- ½ cup chopped walnuts
- ½ cup chopped pecans
- 1 cup crushed potato chips
- ½ cup toffee bits - *these are sold in bags, like
  chocolate chips. But if you can't find them, just
  chop up your favorite candy bar*
- ½ cup white chocolate chips
- ½ cup butterscotch chips
- ½ cup coconut
- 2 14-ounce cans of sweetened condensed milk

1. Preheat oven to 350°F. Coat a 9x13" brownie pan with
pan spray.

2. Combine pretzels, graham crackers, and sugar in a
food processor and pulse to create crumbs. Add the melted butter and pulse again until just combined. Press
this mixture evenly into the bottom of the prepared pan.

3. Begin layering the remaining ingredients as evenly as
possible. Spread out the chocolate chips, walnuts, pecans, potato chips, toffee, white and butterscotch
chips, and coconut. Drizzle the sweetened condensed milk
over it all as evenly as possible. Don't forget to cover
the edges, which tend to be left dry. Bake for 30
minutes, until golden and bubbly. Cool for 10 minutes,
then cut into bars. (Cutting is easier if they are still
a little warm.)

I Loaf you all the Thyme
(I Love You All the Time, *Zipper Down,* 2015)

This **Lemon-Thyme Butter Cake** can be used either to impress your friends or eat your feelings—or both. Serve it with a dollop of clotted cream at high tea, or a fifth of Jack Daniels any fucking time you want.

Ingredients

- Grated zest and juice of 1 large lemon
- 1 cup granulated sugar
- 2 tablespoons fresh thyme — *pick the nice leaves off. No stems ya lazy fuck.*
- 6 tablespoons (3 ounces, or ¾ stick) unsalted butter
- 4 large eggs
- 2 cups all-purpose flour
- 1 teaspoon baking powder
- ½ teaspoon sea salt
- ¾ cup buttermilk
- ½ cup marmalade
- ½ cup orange juice
- Powdered sugar for dusting

Method

1. Preheat oven to 350°F. Coat an 8x4(ish) rectangular loaf pan with pan spray. Dust the sprayed pan with flour, and tap out the excess.

2. Grate the lemon zest using a Microplane. (*This tool is nothing but a carpenter's rasp with a handle on it. Alternatively you can use the finest holes on a box grater. But do not, under any circumstances use a zester! The zester is a stupid fucking tool. It is the Paris Hilton of kitchen equipment. I hate it so much. It wastes half the fruit, and after using it you still have to chop the zest, unless you like eating worm-shaped food.*) Anyway, combine the zest, thyme, and a tablespoon of the sugar in a coffee bean grinder or food processor and pulse until the sugar turns yellow. Then mix it in with the rest of the sugar. If you're too young to have real kitchen tools, you can omit the grinding and just mix them all up.

3. Cream the butter and the delicious lemon-thyme sugar until it is smooth and lump free, then add the eggs, one at a thyme. (See what I did there?)

4. Whisk together the flour, baking powder, and salt. Combine the buttermilk and lemon juice. Add the flour mixture to the butter mixture alternately with the milk — in about 3 increments. Mix well, but don't mix it to death. Transfer the batter to the prepared pan and bake it for about 45 minutes. It will be done when a pick inserted in the center comes out clean, not all batter-y. (Baking time varies depending on your pan, your oven, your intelligence—you'll have to use your eyes and check it a few times.) Let cool for 5 minutes, then turn it out onto a plate.

5. Combine the marmalade and orange juice in a small saucepan and heat to a simmer, stirring. Drizzle this warm glaze over your beautiful cake. It should seep in a bit. Let it cool, then finish it off with a dusting of powdered sugar. It's pretty good with a plop of whipped cream and some fresh berries, too. You'll love this all the time.

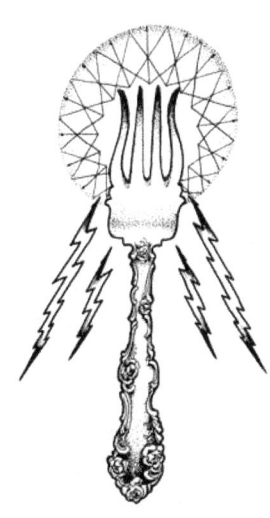

The Food of Our Friends

The following recipes and food memories were generously
shared by several survivors of the Bataclan.
It is a reminder to us all that living a full and
delicious life is the best defense.

Camembert au Beurre Aillé

"This cooking book reminded me of Renaud (Le Guen), my
brother-in-law killed in the Bataclan, because he used to cook a
very specific and delicious dish called "camembert au beurre
aillé". I think it was a recipe he created himself, because I have
never seen it anywhere else! It is made with typically French
ingredients, and may be quite difficult to cook in the US. The
first and main ingredient is a camembert (a French cheese that
smells a lot :) Renaud put it in a pan, so that the cheese start-
ed to melt a little and glaze. Then, the camembert was put 30
seconds in the microwave until completely soft. Finally, it was
covered with melted butter. (No, it is not recommended if
you're on a diet!). It is a special kind of butter we use in France
to stuff snails called "beurre aillé" or "beurre persillé". It con-
tains garlic ("ail" in French) and parsley ("persil" in
French).Serve this as a side dish or with a simple salad, or, if
you really want to live the complete experience, pan-fried potatoes :) This was just one of the many ways Renaud pleased his
family and friends. The Eagles of Death Metal was one of its
favorite bands, and we were all very happy to go to this concert."
-    Laura Toubin

*Thank you Laura! By the way, we have Camembert in Ameri-
ca—and butter and garlic and parsley. We also now have
clogged arteries, thanks you and Renaud. Rock On!*

Mousse au Chocolat

"One of my strongest food memories is of a French dessert
called Mousse au Chocolat. As far back as I can remember, my
mother always made it on special occasions such as birthdays
or Christmas. Over time, it became a classic of her cuisine. Her
recipe came from the back of Nestlé dark chocolate bars, and it
is child's play to make. All you need is 200g (7 ounces) of dark
chocolate, 6 eggs and a pinch of salt. Here are the steps: Melt

the chocolate in a bain-marie and let it cool down. Separate the eggs. Add salt in the whites and whip them to stiff peaks. In a separate bowl, beat together the yolks and chocolate. Carefully fold 1/3 of the whipped whites into the yolks. Add remaining whites and fold thoroughly but carefully, so as not to deflate the whites. Chill for at least 3 hours. You can serve it in ramekins with a mint leaf on top or add some cinnamon. It should serve 8 people. Bon appétit !"
   -   From Arthur Pujol

Thank you Arthur – There is nothing better than a good chocolate mousse. If I am not mistaken, Escoffier got his recipe off the back of a Nestlés chocolate bar too.

Chicken Korma

"To me, food is above all a means of bringing people together. The best meals enhance an already great moment. One of my best friends has a house in the French countryside that we would visit often. Many different people were invited over the years to relax, play games, and listen to the great music collection. All this fun was interrupted by delicious cooking sessions. The most memorable dish, without a doubt, was my friend's "Chicken Korma." It starts with coriander, ginger, chili and onions cooked in olive oil. Add to that the korma paste, chicken, chickpeas, and coconut milk. Simmer it for 45 minutes, then serve on top of rice. Top it with hot chiles, almonds, yogurt, and lime juice. It's as hot as a Kyuss record, and sweet as the best Mogwai songs."
   -   From Valentin Gillet

Thanks Valentin. I was already on board at "korma", but you totally sold it with the last line.

Gratin Dauphinois

"Food has always been important in my life. My grandmother said the people who love cooking and eating good food are the only ones that really enjoy life. It used to make me laugh, but now I understand what she meant. We would cook together for hours, and she told me about her incredible life. Today, when I cook those dishes, I feel her standing by my side, and it makes food taste so much better! She often made "gratin Dauphinois", a typical French dish with potatoes and cream. It's easy, fast, cheap and delicious! You need 1.5 kg of

potatoes (3.3 pounds), 3 garlic cloves, 40 cl of sour cream (1.5 cups), 1L of milk (4.2 cups), 100 g of butter (3.5 ounces), salt, pepper and nutmeg. Peel, wash and thinly slice the potatoes. Bring to boil the milk, garlic, salt, pepper, nutmeg. Add the potatoes and let it cook for 10 to 15 minutes. Spread the butter in an ovenproof dish, arrange the potatoes, top with cream, add little bit of butter, salt and pepper. Bake for 50 minutes at 180°C (356°F). You can serve it with a fine meat, or just a green salad. Enjoy !"
-   From Camille Simien

Thank you Camille. In the United States we call this scalloped potatoes, and though we teach it in culinary schools, it is also available dehydrated in a box at Walmart. Not that any self-respecting culinarian would buy such a thing—unless the munchies were really bad.

<u>And last, but certainly not least</u>

When Jesse was born, his paternal grandparents, Charles and Jo Hughes, were the proprietors of a diner called "THE DUNEAN CAFE". After Poppa Hughes' death, it came to be known as "Jo's Cafe". The family would all love to hang out there because the place attracted all the local characters, so full of life. Jesse especially loved being there, sitting on a stool at the counter, watching his Poppa at the grill. Poppa had his own secret recipe for Barbecue Pork, and there was a daily special consisting of a meat entree and 2 vegetables, served with cornbread - all very Southern.
Jesse always liked most food, with the exception of carrots. The one time I made him taste a carrot at the table, he immediately 'illustrated' that it wasn't going to stay down. Needless to say, I never forced him to taste anything again. As a kid in Palm Desert Middle School, his favorite snack was a bread sandwich, consisting of three slices of bread that Jesse would smash into a ball before he ate it. I guess he's always been creative!
-JoEllen Hughes, Mom to Jesse Hughes
& Eagles of Death Metal

Conversion Tables

Measurement Equivalents

1 1/2 teaspoon=1/2 tablespoon=		1/4 fluid ounce
3 teaspoon=	1 tablespoon=	1/2 fluid ounce
1 tablespoon=	3 teaspoon=	1/2 fluid ounce
2 tablespoon=	1/8 cup=	1 fluid ounce
4 tablespoon=	1/4 cup=	2 fluid ounces
8 tablespoon=	1/2 cup=	4 fluid ounces
12 tablespoon=	3/4 cup=	6 fluid ounces
16 tablespoon=	1 cup=	8 fluid ounces
1 cup=	16 tablespoon=	8 fluid ounces
2 cups=	1 pint=	16 fluid ounces
4 cups=	2 pint=	32 fluid ounces= 1 qt
16 cups=	4 quart=	128 fluid ounces= 1 gal

Temperature

To convert Fahrenheit to Celsius,
subtract 32, divide by 9, multiply by 5.

To convert Celsius to Fahrenheit,
divide by 5, multiply by 9, add 32.

Fahrenheit	Celsius	
32°F	0°C	(Freezing)
50°F	10°C	
100°F	37.8°C	
120°F	48.9°C	
150°F	65.6°C	
200°F	93.3°C	
212°F	100°C (Boiling)	
240°F	115°C (Soft Ball)	
250°F	121°C (Hard Ball)	
270°F	132°C (Soft Crack)	
300°F	149°C (Hard Crack)	
320°F	160°C (Caramel)	
350°F	177°C	
400°F	205°C	
450°F	233°C	
500°F	260°C	

Weight

To convert ounces to grams, multiply by 28.35
To convert grams into ounces, multiply by 0.03527
Kilograms into pounds, multiply by 2.2046

When multiplying large weight,
round to nearest whole number

US	Metric(approximate)
1/2 ounces	15 grams
2/3 ounces	20 grams
3/4 ounces	22 grams
1 ounce	30 grams
2 ounces	55 grams
4 ounces (1/4 pound)	115 grams
5 ounces	140 grams
8 ounces (1/2 pound)	225 grams
12 ounces	340 grams
16 ounces (1 pound)	455 grams
2 pounds	910 grams
3 pounds	1 kilogram,365 grams
4 pounds	1 kilogram,820 grams
5 pounds	2 kilogram,275 grams

Volume

To convert milliliters into ounces, multiply by 0.0338
To convert milliliters into pints, multiply by 0.0021125
To convert liters into ounces, multiply by 33.8
To convert liters into pints, multiply by 2.1125
To convert liters into quarts, multiply by 1.05625
To convert quarts into liters, multiply by 0.946

When multiplying large volume,
round to nearest whole number

US	Metric (approximate)
1/2 teaspoon	2.5 milliliter
1 teaspoon	5 milliliter
1 tablespoon	15 milliliter
1 cup	237 milliliter
1 pint	475 milliliter
1 quart	950 milliliter

Length

To convert inches into centimeters,
multiply by 2.54

To convert centimeters into inches,
multiply by 0.3937

To convert meters into inches,
multiply by 39.3701

Thanks to Dissention Records and Artist Management for their generous support.

CPSIA information can be obtained
at www.ICGtesting.com
Printed in the USA
FSOW04n2343261016
26622FS